Rev. Robert
June 11, 1

from
Mrs. Helen Holmes

Life's
Extras

ARCHIBALD RUTLEDGE

FLEMING H. REVELL COMPANY

For Florence,
my life's best extra

Introduction

ARCHIBALD RUTLEDGE is one of those rare souls who see sermons in stones and books in brooks and the bright light of God over everything. Across a reverently gay and gentle lifetime he has had eyes to see and ears to hear music which most of us miss, and he describes the music in this little book.

He writes of the glorious extras of life, the deeply spiritual extras, half-hidden for the seeker to find in the bottomless bounty of nature —moonlight and mockingbirds, rainbows, the colors on the Creator's palette splashed spendthrift in the skies of dawn and sunset, the rift in the storm clouds with the sun breaking through, chaos becoming celestial message—

INTRODUCTION

life's extras! None of it, to this man so aware of God, is "accident of nature": it is instead the handiwork, the will, the love of God.

"I know," he says, "that the spiritual luxuries we so freely enjoy vindicate the faith that behind the Veil is the God of mercy and of tenderest love." The pages of the little book have become the most popular he has written—perhaps because with so gentle a hand and a heart so filled, he has drawn open the curtain, for just a moment, that we might see God. This is the aim and the artistry of *Life's Extras*.

THE PUBLISHERS

Contents

THE MYSTERY OF

LIFE'S EXTRAS

MY CASUAL ACQUAINTANCE on the train that was speeding across the autumn landscape seemed thoughtful, reflective, a little wistful as we talked about the things we saw from the car window. At last we came to a big meadow wherein were grazing half a hundred beef cattle. I said something inane about the prosperity of the country, the glowing future of the live-stock industry, and so forth. "Look at

11

those little daisies," he said, pointing to a bright patch of them in a far corner of the meadow. Then he added, "Cattle somehow can't thrill me. There's more hope for humanity in a wild flower than in tons of beef."

Long after he left me, I kept thinking of what he had said, wondering just what he had meant. His idea, of course, was that a wild flower is one of life's extras, one of those things that we do not *have* to have but which we enjoy all the more for that very reason.

The more I thought about this, the more it appeared that Creation supplies us with only two kinds of things: necessities and extras. Sunlight, air, water, food, shelter— these are among the bare necessities. With them we can exist. But moonlight and starlight are distinctly extras; so are music, the perfumes, flowers. The wind is perhaps a necessity; but the song that it croons through the morning pines is a different thing.

The fascinating part about all this is not the tabulating of life's necessities and life's extras; it is rather the question, Who put them here, and for what purpose? Furthermore, shall we not find, through some stories of personal experience, that the curious and significant remark of my casual acquaintance was right? I do not presume that my actual living this mortal life has in any way been unique, especially as regards this matter of life's extras; yet, if I can tell what they have meant to me, I shall perhaps be voicing the experience and the hope of many.

I remember one October night visiting a friend who was lying very sick. There was a full moon that night; and as I walked down the village street on my sad mission I felt the silvery beauty of it quiet my heart. The world lay lustrous. There was no scrawny bush nor ugly clod that was not transfigured in that glory. A little breeze over the brimming salt tide brought aromatic marshy odors. It seemed to me that some power was trying to make beauty take away my sadness. I found my friend not less aware than I was of the beauty of the night. He could look from his window and see the argent glamour of it all: how it flooded the gleaming tide with celestial lights; how it ran long white lances through the swarthy cedars; how it tinged with soft radiance the locusts and the mimosas. He felt the breeze too, and delighted in the odours that it brought of the happy world beyond his window.

THE GUIDANCE OF

THE HEART

AT ANY RATE, I know that a thoughtful consideration of life's extras has done more to give my faith in God actual conviction than all the sermons I ever heard. My knowledge of theology is hardly more ample than that of a bushman of Borneo; but I am absolutely unshaken in my faith that God created us, loves us, and wants us not only to be good but to be happy. He ministers to our bodies by the necessities that abound in the world; and to our spirits by the beauty that adorns creation. One has no difficulty in discovering, in the vast scheme of things, an extraordinary, an exciting, provision and prevision. As philosophy, I know not if this will stand; but I do know that a belief in it has brought me close to God.

I cannot regard the "fiery funeral of foliage old" as accidental, nor the gorgeous pageantry of sunset as anything but the manifestation of divine art. I stood recently on the shores of a mountain lake at sundown after a heavy rain, and watched for an hour the magnificence of the west; the huge clouds smoldering, the long lanes of emerald light between them, then isolated clouds like red roses climbing up some oriel window of the sky, the deep refulgence behind it all. Superb as it was, momently it changed, so that I saw in reality a score of sunsets. I looked across the lonely, limpid lake, past the dark forest, far into the heart of the flaming, fading skies. I was sure that God had done that; moreover, that He had done it for a purpose. When did He ever do anything idly? And what was the purpose? Surely to fill the hearts of His children with a sense of beauty and of awe, and to teach them of His loving care.

Neither a day-dawning nor a sunset (with all its attendant beauty) is really a necessity. It is one of life's extras. It is a visit to an incomparable art gallery; and no one has to pay any admission fee. The human mind, being somewhat proud and perverse, may be inclined to reject this kind of proof of God's love. But the human heart can hardly do so. And in things spiritual I do not know but that the heart is by far the better guide.

RHODODENDRONS AND

SAPPHIRE SKIES

NOT LONG AGO, I visited a lonely cabin in the North Carolina mountains, whence the owner had just been taken, charged with murder. He and a neighbor had had a fatal altercation about a line fence, and he had "drawn" more quickly than the other. The accused had borne a good reputation up to this time. Both men had seen service in France. I was rather well acquainted with both families.

LIFE'S EXTRAS

As I went up the old gullied mountain road toward the home of the first, I noticed in the wild glen, down which a white stream gurgled and spurted, incessant, vehement, and joyous, that the rhododendrons were in blossom. There may be a more beautiful flower, but I have not seen it—taking it all in all, and considering the wildwood setting in which it invariably grows. To look at this wondrous flower and not to feel that God exquisitely designed it, and did it not merely as a vagrant artist but with precision and nobility of purpose is to me incredible. Ere long I reached the cabin, and one of the man's sisters greeted me and talked with me. Over the humble mantel I saw a crude little photograph of him in his uniform; and beside it, in a small bottle that functioned as a vase, I saw a sprig of rhododendron blossom. I looked at the picture; then I said something casual about the flower.

"I don't know why," my hostess said, "but to have it there helps me. It 'minds me of God."

I have always loved the eloquence of simple people. What they say, coming from the heart, often goes straight to the heart. "It 'minds me of God." I never see a rhododendron without remembering that. And

29

are not all of life's extras reminders of the love and the yearning compassion of God?

I mentioned sunsets and sunrises as extras. Almost the whole complex and wonderful matter of color in the world seems as extra. The color of the sky might have been a dingy gray, or a painful yellow, or a plum-colored purple. But it is sapphire; and my philosophy makes me believe that such a color for the sky is by no means the result of mere chance. Granted that it is the result of the operation of certain laws, forces, and conditions; yet behind it all, back of the realized dream, is the mighty intelligence of the Creator, the vast amplitude of the dreamer's comprehension. And let us not forget that the two colors at which we can gaze longest are blue and green. There is about them a coolness, a serenity, a spirit of fragrant peace. And as the blue prevails in the sky, the green does upon earth.

THE SEN

I HAVE OFTEN heard people say that they would like to remake the world. Well, I am glad that we don't have to live in a man-made world. If we consider merely the least of the marvelous provisions for our comfort and our happiness, we can realize how impossible would be an earth and a scheme of life that man had made. And we should feel, also, that David was

35

right: "For as the heaven is high above the earth, so great is His mercy toward them that fear Him." How high is the heaven? Illimitable. And so is God's love.

To a sophisticated person, this sort of belief may seem too childlike. Yet I have the gravest suspicions of sophistication. I have never discovered it in nature; and to me it seems that instead of being a proof of enlightenment and culture, it is the evidence rather of ignorance, and perhaps of folly. It is the triumph of shallowness and sterility. The real trouble with a sophisticated person is not that he knows too much, but that he knows too little.

LIFE'S EXTRAS

Probably everyone has had some kind of experience with a star, or with the stars. I mean that, at some moment, a star has risen, or has been seen, or has set amid circumstances that made the memory of it a part of one's life. I remember that the morning star I used to see blazing above the plantation pines, when I was up early to feed the stock, or to be about some other work, used to thrill me with the beauty of its startling radiance. It seemed all dewy and throbbing —a thing alive, glorious and immortal. God set it there, I felt, as a reminder of His presence, so that we might begin our day with the thought of Him. So when the

evening came, a great beacon of the twi-
light reminds us of Him again. Our days
and nights are sentineled by the splendid
warders of God.

STARLIGHT THROUGH

THE STORM

I ONCE HAD a curious experience with a star. I was driving home to the plantation, in the old motorless days, when I was overtaken at dusk by a storm of hurricane violence. Inky darkness shrouded the world. I could not even see the road ahead or behind. The thunder and lightning were appalling. Finally, a bolt struck a pine not twenty feet from my buggy. My horse had stood a good deal from this storm; but now he made a sudden dash. He broke away through the forest, and I could not hold him. In a moment he had run between two pines standing close together, had smashed both shafts, and had torn loose from the buggy and from me. Into the howling darkness he vanished.

The rain came down as if it meant to make a joke of the Flood. The thunder blared. The lightning became most uncomfortably intimate and intrusive. I heard near me great trees go crashing down in the fury of the tempest. Alone I was, defenseless, in profound darkness. I knew in a way where I was, and to locate myself the better I looked toward what I believed to be the west.

Through the heavy arras of the rain, to my amazement, I saw a little rift in the storm-rack, hardly bigger than my hand, in the very heart of which the evening star gleamed in dewy-silver solitude. In all the stillness of felicity it shone serenely, saying to my heart, "This storm is an imposter. It is momentary. The sky is here, and the stars; all shall be well."

Amid all the desolation about me, and the seemingly hopeless chaos, here came a celestial message. Shining through the storm-rack, its light reminded me of something past our world. Taking heart, I waded out to the road, found my horse waiting for me half a mile down its gleaming length, rode homeward through the breaking storm, and reached the house in full, calm starlight. Stars fill me with a sense of God; and the heart cannot help being grateful when it remembers that the beauty and the wonder of them may be accounted things not to enable us to exist, but gifts of love to make us joyous.

If there is anything in life in which I take a pardonable pride, it is in my friendship for certain old woodsmen and hunters;

obscure men, as far as the world is concerned, but faithful friends, loyal comrades. Occasionally one will tell me something intimate about himself; and when he does it is usually remarkable, as I believe the following story is. I shall give it without embellishment.

"It happened last June," my friend told me, as we were sitting together on a pine log in the depths of a virgin forest. "I tell it to you because I know if you tell it, you will never use my name. Bill Moore and I, you see, had had trouble between us for years. The last time we met in town, if friends hadn't separated us we would have finished the thing right there. A lot of things had made us feel as we did; and everything that happened appeared to make it worse.

"After that night in town, I figured that one of us would get the other. I knew he always carried a gun, and I began to do the same. Well, that day in June one of the field hands told me that Bill said he would get me. I made up my mind to meet him a little more than halfway, and late that afternoon I rode up toward Bill's house, about three miles from mine, intending to have the thing over. A man can't live in that kind of suspense.

THE MESSAGE OF THE

WHITE BAY FLOWER

"**Y**OU'LL THINK I was a fool, but that flower set me to thinking about my mother, and about them old days, and about the kind of man she hoped I might be when she was gone. The first thing I knew the man on horseback was right opposite me in the road. And it was Bill, all right.

"But in the few minutes he had taken to come up, something had happened to me. I didn't want to harm him now. I didn't feel that I had to look out for myself. Perhaps I did a risky thing, but I rode out of the bushes, calling to him. Something in the way I came up made him know it was all right. And it was all right, 'cause we made it up right there and then; and we are better friends than ever we were before anything happened. Now what do you think of that —and all because of a little white flower? But it's all the truth, just as I'm telling you."

He "redeemeth thy life from destruction," says the Psalmist; but we do not often think of the deft and beautiful ways in which God works. Beauty is made to touch the heart, a right spirit is renewed, and the life is redeemed. I don't think this is preaching; I hope not, for of all men I am the least capable or worthy to undertake that. It just seems to me like a rehearsal of truth. Surely life's extras not only give us happiness in a positive way but also indirectly: by saving us from the tragic loss of our nobler instincts, they rescue us in times of peril.

There are very few sounds in the natural world that are harsh. Even the massive rolling of thunder has about it something of solemn beauty. In anthems the sea rolls on the beach; and in the sunny shallows there are water-harps forever making melodies. The wind is a chorister. Many a wild bird can warble like an aerial rivulet. The world is really a melodious place, full of soft sounds and harmony. Man makes it riotous and blatant.

I remember being especially impressed with this truth when I went one day into the forest to try to escape from a grief that had come to me—the loss of one dearly beloved.

THE ONE BEHIND

THE VEIL

A LITTLE WAY within the borders of that fragrant, dewy forest, where giant yellow pines, tall as the masts of brigantines and full of dim contralto music in their crowns, rejoiced in the sunshine—just here I heard a parula-warbler singing. He was in the crest of a bald cypress, high over the dreamy waters of a little woodland lake. The bird's song sounded like a delicate astral flute, sounded softly and sweetly, to lure me out of my trouble. High in the heavenly blue this chorister was, joyous in that halcyon repose that the heart enjoys when it is at peace. Like a voice of a spirit was this music; it came to me calmly yet thrillingly. Like a quieting hand was that beautiful song, to cool the fever of care, to still the pulse's leap.

All about me were the rejoicing looks of the flowers, and the shining hush and loveliness of dew-hung ferns and bushes, and the gentle, pure passion of the sunlight. And music there was from myriads of sources: gossamer lyrics from bees; the laughter of a little stream jesting with the roots of a mighty pine. The wind's soft wand touched the tall grasses and the sweet myrtles into a sibilant elfin choir. Everywhere I looked I saw wild, sequestered grace. The great pines chanted like the sea, their harps of the sky touched like things celestial. And what did the music and the beauty, those extras, bring me? Passing from a state of keenest grief I came to one of quiet reconcilement—to the profound conviction that, living or dying, God will take care of us.

God seemed very near to me in that wood; the beauty of it all trembled with

His grace; the music held His voice. I saw there both life and death—in the green leaves and the brown, in the standing trees and the fallen. If one is honest with himself when he asks the question, What is it that perishes? he will be obliged to answer, Everything that the eye sees. In the forest, amid those things that God provided, I came to understand that if we are to hold anything—and in times of sorrow we *must* have something to which we can cling—it must be to the unseen.

For the strength that is permanent, we have to lean on visions; for immortal hope, we have to trust, not the things that we perceive but those invisible things that our spirits affirm.

I remember walking early one July morning down a thickety path. Trees completely overarched it; but far ahead light gleamed. The path was long and straight, and terminated in a wide meadow. As I glanced upward, my eye caught sight of what I supposed to be a knot on the end of a dead limb that hung directly over the pathway; it was clearly silhouetted against the sky line ahead. In a moment something had darted over my head and had alighted on the knot. It was a hummingbird on its nest, which hung like a fairy bassinet in the lonely woodland. I looked at the nest and at the bird, with its elfin grace, its delicate sheen of brilliance, its jeweled throat. And I thought: This whole matter of *grace,* of elegance, of delicacy and felicity of beauty is an extra. It is not necessary to have it so. But God has willed it so, because He loves us and knows our hungry hearts need this kind of beauty.

For many years, I had an idea that nature had for man an active sympathy; but now I have changed my opinion. There seems really a superb indifference about nature. It is what lies behind nature that really has sympathy. The rose does not of itself bloom for us; but God has made it to bloom for us. Surely this beauty is not a random affair; it is too authentically a sign and symbol of love. All we know about the highest form of affection we have learned directly from God's affection for us. We not only "love Him because He first loved us," but we love one another because He teaches us how. We originate with Him; and our sublimest art is nothing but attempts to imitate the things in nature that He has created.

Whatever my religion may be worth, I feel deeply that life's extras have given it to me; and time shall not take it from me.

Meditating on what we have, not merely to sustain us but to make us joyous and serene in life, I have come to so clear a consciousness of God that of all men the atheist appears to me the most pitiable and foolish. Nor have I come to this faith by roseate paths alone. I know well the Valley of the Shadow; I know the aspect of that Veil which mortal sight cannot pierce. But I know, also, that the spiritual luxuries that we so freely enjoy vindicate the faith that behind the Veil is the God of mercy and of tenderest love.